A STEMINIST FORCE

LAURA W CarteR
&
ANNA DohERty

Published by Familius LLC, www.familius.com
PO Box 1249, Reedley, CA 93654

Familius books are available at special discounts for bulk purchases, whether for sales promotions or
for family or corporate use. For more information, contact Familius Sales at orders@familius.com.

Library of Congress Control Number: 2023947273

Print ISBN 9781641709606
EPUB ISBN 9781641708654
Kindle ISBN 9781641708647
Fixed PDF ISBN 9781641708630

Printed in China

Edited by Brooke Jorden
Cover design by Anna Doherty
Book design by Brooke Jorden

10 9 8 7 6 5 4 3 2 1

First Edition

A STEMINIST FORCE

LAURA W CarteR & ANNA DohErty

STEAM!

We are girls as bright as fire!
We're a STEMINIST brigade
leaving blazing trails behind us
on our groundbreaking crusade.

We are human calculators,
perfect mathematician queens.

We are programmers designing
codes and apps for your machines.

We are astronauts who reach for stars that shine in outer space.

And we're physicists who measure how things move from place to place.

MAE JEMISON

KALPANA CHAWLA

KATHERINE JOHNSON

GIRL PWR!

WANGARI MAATHAI

We are conservationists
who care and fight for Mother Earth.

And as therapists, we help people
remember they have worth.

JANE ADDAMS

BERTA ISABEL
CÁCERES FLORES

JOYCE BROTHERS

ANNA COMSTOCK

STEMINISTS!

INSOO KIM BERG

We are doctors healing patients
and researching new vaccines.

MARIA ANDRADE

EVANGELINA VILLEGAS

We are farmers tilling soil and
growing wheat and corn and greens.

MICHIYO TSUJIMURA

We are teachers shaping young minds
so they learn and think and grow.

We are writers crafting stories,
changing what readers think they know.

We're marine biologists
who study life beneath the waves.

ROSA
MABEL
LEE

MARIA
DE LOS
ANGELES
ALVARINO
GONZALES

SYLVIA EARLE

We're geologists who travel
to the deepest of Earth's caves.

We're creative engineers
designing shuttles that can fly.

We're meteorologists
tracking storms across the sky.

EUNICE FOOTE

JUNE BACON-BERCY

STEM GANG

STEMINISTS!

We are architects who draft plans for new buildings, small and grand.

ELISABETH SCOTT

NORMA MERRICK SKLAREK

MARION MAHONY GRIFFIN

We are archeologists
who search for bones beneath the sand.

We are marching
hand in hand.

We refuse to stop or fail.

We are rising up together,
and together, we'll prevail.

We are talented and smart.
We are charting a new course.

And history will record us
as a fierce STEMINIST force.

Mathematicians

- Sofia Kovalevskaya (1850-1891) – 1st woman in Europe to receive a PhD in Math (Russian)
- Dorothy Vaughan (1910-2008) – African-American woman who was NASA's "human calculator"
- Maryam Mirzakhani (1977-2017)– won the prestigious Fields Medal in Math (Iranian)

Programers/Coders

- Grace Hopper (1906-1992) – co-developed COBOL, an early computer-programming language (American)
- Karen Spärck Jones (1935-2007) – helped develop Inverse Document Frequency that's used in most search engines (British)

Astronauts

- Chiaki Mukai (1952-present) – 1st Japanese woman in space
- Sally Ride (1951-2012) – 1st American woman in space
- Mae Jemison (1956-present) – 1st African-American woman in space
- Kalpana Chawla (1962-2003) – 1st woman of Indian descent in space

Physicists

- Marie Curie (1867-1934) – 1st woman to receive Nobel Prize; worked on radioactivity (Polish/French)
- Ruby Payne Scott (1912-1981) – 1st female radio astronomer; her work led to the discovery of black holes (Australian)
- Katherine Johnson (1918-2020) – NASA physicist and mathematician who calculated trajectories needed for space flight (African American)

Conservationists

- Anna Comstock (1854-1930) – naturalist and pioneer in natural studies; wrote *The Handbook of Nature Study* (American)
- Wangari Maathai (1940-2011) – founder of the Green Belt Movement to fight deforestation; received the Nobel Peace Prize in 2004 (Kenyan)
- Berta Isabel Caceres Flores (1971-2016) – environmental activist who co-founded the Council of Popular and Indigenous Organizations of Honduras to advocate for the native Lenca people of Honduras (Honduran)

Therapists

- Jane Addams (1860-1935) — suffragette, social worker, and peace advocate who founded the influential Hull House in Chicago; 2nd woman to receive the Nobel Peace Prize (American)
- Dr. Joyce Brothers (1927-2013) — pioneer of "pop" psychology who used television programs and newspaper columns to provide advice and advocate for mental health (American)
- Insoo Kim Berg (1934-2007) — psychotherapist and co-founder of Solution-Focused Brief Therapy (Korean-American)

Physicians

- Rebecca Lee Crumpler (1831-1895) — 1st African-American woman to receive a medical degree
- Susan La Flesche Picotte (1865-1915) — advocate for public health of Native Americans and the 1st Native American woman to receive a medical degree
- Yoshioka Yayoi (1871-1959) — physician and educator who founded the Tokyo Women's Medical University (Japanese)
- Helen Taussig (1898-1986) - founded the field of pediatric cardiology (American)

Farmers

- Maria Andrade (1958-present) – food scientist and plant-genetic specialist who researches and creates drought-tolerant varieties of sweet potatoes (Cape Verdean)
- Evangelina Villegas (1924-2017) – biochemist who researched and created more nutrient-dense varieties of maize (Mexican)
- Michiyo Tsujimura (1888-1969) – agricultural scientist and biochemist who researched chemical components of green tea (Japanese)

Teachers

- Savitribia Phule (1831-1897) – 1st female teacher in India and the mother of Indian feminism
- Maria Montessori (1870-1952) – physician and educator who developed the "Montessori Method" of education (Italian)
- Alice Freeman Palmer (1855-1902) – educator and the 2nd female president of Wellesley College; champion of women's university education (American)

Writers

- Phillis Wheatley (1753-1784) – West-African woman who was enslaved in Massachusetts from c.1760-1773; became the 1st published African-American poet in American history with her book, *Poems on Various Subjects, Religious and Moral*
- Mary Wollstonecraft (1759-1797) – early feminist and author of *A Vindication of the Rights of Woman* (British)

- Mary Shelley (1797-1851) — author of *Frankenstein*, which made her one of the first science fiction novelists (English)
- Rachel Carson (1907-1964) — author of *Silent Spring*, a book that launched the modern environmental movement (American)

Marine Biologists
- Sylvia Earle (1935-present) — prominent marine biologist who was the 1st woman to walk the ocean floor (American)
- María de los Ángeles Alvariño González (1916-2005) — studied plankton and discovered 22 new species of marine animals (Spanish)
- Rosa Mabel Lee (1884-1976) — discovered the "Rosa Lee Phenomena" by which the age of fish can be determined by studying the rings on their scales (British)

Geologists
- Marie Tharp (1920-2006) — oceanic cartographer who helped create the first map of the Atlantic Ocean floor (American)
- Florence Bascom (1862-1945) — 1st American female geologist; researched volcanic rocks
- Inge Lehmann (1888-1993) — physicist credited with discovering Earth's solid inner core and molten outer core (Danish)

Engineers

- Hedy Lamarr (1914-2000) – helped develop frequency-hopping technology that paved the way for wireless communication technology like Wi-Fi (Austrian-American)
- Ellen Ochoa (1958-present) – engineer and inventor who worked on optical and imaging technology; also the 1st Hispanic-American woman in space
- Edith Clarke (1883-1959) – 1st professional female electrical engineer in the United States; worked on A-C power circuits and hydroelectric dams (American)
- Emily Warren Roebling (1843-1903) – engineer who helped design the Brooklyn Bridge (American)

Meteorologists

- Eunice Newton Foote (1819-1888) – researched greenhouse effect of sunlight on certain gasses (American)
- June Bacon-Bercey (1923-2010) – 1st African-American female meteorologist and 1st female TV meteorologist

Architects

- Marion Mahony Griffin (1871-1961) – one of the first licensed female architects in the world; helped develop Prairie-style architecture with Frank Lloyd Wright (American)
- Elisabeth Scott (1898-1972) – renowned architect who designed the Shakespeare Memorial Theater in England (British)
- Norma Merrick Sklarek (1926-2012) – one of the first female African-American architects; designed the US Embassy in Tokyo and other notable sites

Archeologists

- Dame Maud Cunnington (1869-1951) – archaeologist who helped excavate historic sites, such as Stonehenge and Woodenhenge (Welsh)
- Gertrude Bell (1868-1926) – archaeologist who researched former Ottoman Empire sites in Syria and Iraq (British)
- Dorothy Garrod (1892-1968) – archaeologist who specialized in the Paleolithic Era of human history (British)